Meandering Musings

Sophia Kunkel

BookLeaf
Publishing

India | USA | UK

Presentation by *BookLeaf Publishing*

Web: www.bookleafpub.com

E-mail: info@bookleafpub.com

ISBN: 9789358319729

First edition 2022

DEDICATION

To Mama, Papa, Nathan, and Alex

ACKNOWLEDGEMENT

My first and deepest thanks goes to God for instilling the passion for writing inside my heart. I never thought I would be able to pursue poetry, but He granted me with the determination and inspiration to do so.

Secondly, thank you to Bookleaf Publishing for providing this unique opportunity! I have loved every minute of it!

Also, thank you to all my friends and family who have been endlessly supportive of me and my writing journey. Y'all are the reason I continue to seek out ways to expand and broaden my craft!

Shout-out to Francesca Kyanda, my partner in crime during this project. I'm not sure I could have finished all 21 days of the challenge if not for your encouragement and motivation. Thank you for being such a great friend!

PREFACE

"You can never get a cup of tea large enough or
a book long enough to suit me."
- C.S. Lewis.

I Wonder If

change is a leaf dancing in the quickening wind,
   partaking in an annual migration to nowhere
  and joining the swirling chaos of fiery red and
glowering orange below—
      where remnants of brothers and sisters
lie littered like snow
        because of weary black boots,
traversing as death,
  each step uncertain, but impactful
nonetheless.

Footprints

Blood-stained snow stifles all growth,
hides in crevices and suffocates every shy hope
like thick billowing smog snuffs out the light
and
buries all emotion under punishing white veils
disguising hateful words with beautiful
intentions.

                    Blood-stained snow infects
the land, my home,
                  concealed in razor-sharp
smiles and sickly-sweet lies;
                  a plague of epic proportions
accompanying the first
                  leaves not a single droplet
of beautiful glowing sun.

Then, poking through the ice, is a tendril of
green,
the translucent glow of petals, resistant to the
biting cold;
Bent but not broken under winter's iron grasp
and blooming, in spite of our blood-stained
footprints in the snow.

SORROW

The sky a muted gray
muffled by shadow-eclipsed clouds and
imminent rain, threatens to unleash its glorious
wrath
upon a dead   wintery   scene
to revive lost hopes, forgotten dreams,
bittersweet memories that now only bring pain;
I pray it may heal my grieving heart, silent
bones,
as a timeless battle rages in the depths of my
mind
whether to stay stuck inside winter or move on
to spring,
whether to be the cold that   kills
feeling
or the gentle drizzling rain that restores life.

Unrequited Love

I dreamed that we were standing in the drizzling rain,
under an ashen sky and a cherry red umbrella
so close that our skin brushed against one another
in the heat of the summer.

I dreamed that I was dancing in the pouring rain
and then I was screaming under the stone faced sky
and then I was weeping below the blood-red umbrella
just to pull your disinterested gaze
back to me.

I dreamed that you were choking in the torrential rain,
and then you were shouting into the black abyss above
and then you were howling, throat tattered
like the remnants of the umbrella,
forever broken, forever fractured.

And so I dreamed that we were standing under a rain-speckled sky,

below sorrowful clouds with hands intertwined,
our unrequited love, the greatest romance never
told.

Faith

People ask me about my faith,
why I believe what I believe,
what could have possibly convinced me
to put my trust in a God unseen;
and to that I have no scientific answer,
nothing that makes sense in the laws of the
world,
just my own internal peace
resting in my soul, it unfurled.

block

fingers frozen stiff, frostbitten and sluggish,
    mind a barren tundra   —nothing to
say—
  lips whisper prayers,   unanswered they
return,
      because the pen that writes no secrets
          is a frightful fear to slay.

spring fling

we had our spring flings
with the same group of dates –
circled, slashed, and crossed on our calendars
as matters of life or death;

for years we memorized the way to success
trekking the same path as those who came
before
because to triumph was to sell our souls
for the good of the grade, for the good of the
school.

so we had our spring flings
with the same group of dates,
waited with bated breath
for the acceptance or rejection
that would spark envy or self-hate.

Were the tears worth it?

this is what happens

metal   scraping   metal and
squealing like   death—
        i find myself in the midst of
            ricocheting   debris,
smoke   and heat   and dust
and ash hiss
simultaneous on a cloudless summer day,
pastries flung,   crumpled into
themselves, i cry over cookies and
lost opportunities and the thoughts that intrude,
    to turn back time and hide in shame,
  and wallow in tears because in the end
        there is only me to blame.

Disappointment

Emblazoned like a tattoo against an ocean of a
sky,
a silver cross overlooks the world, the decaying
leaves, the chatter of songbirds
disappearing into the night, the symphony of
voices blended together as
unified screaming, the tendrils of smoke curling
around our throats and
violence, never ceasing.

Blizzard

Are you here,
     as the days grow
     darker, a blizzard
     (I am Everywhere)
of thoughts as I lay in the dark, head
buried against a tear-stained pillow,
my body trembling and shaking?
     (I am the very air
     you breathe)
     Canyousaveme—
     (Without Fail)
     from the
     fracturing
     ice, the waters
     below, f r o m
     m y s e l f ?

Love Is In The Air

12

i once wrote a letter to you
        on a bleeding blue piece of notebook
paper,
        handwriting scrawled in a fit of agony
        as if our crossed paths could be erased
        forever, with a simple hello and goodbye
and signed, love
the girl you never knew—

                        but I never sent
it.

senior year

senior year was:

ohmigoshwhatishappeningwiththeworld
        and why am I not learning
anything on—
        line, drawn in the dirt, how far
am I willing to go
        to sacrifice my mental health for
things like
        college checklists and english
essays and
        summer internships and jobs—

        wow! a puppy! I don't even
sneeze!
        but it's a shame our time
together is numbered as
        dates on the calendar creep
closer, remind me
        that the future waits for no one
and
        I can barely breathe—

now photographs, polaroids, and
pictures

of memories hang above my bed
on my dorm room wall

fragments of life, shouting,
where did you go?

ANXIOUS

the nail scrapes, pokes, and prods
digging into pink, tender skin
burrowing deeper, leaving scars;
and the teeth pull lips taut,
the taste of blood and scabbed
smiles that frown in mirrored reflection;
palms which kiss then fingers that peek
inside the crevices of the hand,
a self-deceptive self-massage.

Constellation

Did you think I could break so easily,
      that with a simple no, my spirit would
burst
      like a looming rain cloud?

      Did you think I left my heart so
unguarded
      that it would stop beating, dead, after
      you told me I would never amount to
      anything at all?

      Did you think the tears I wept
were a sign of weakness?

      Because you were wrong.

      I am a constellation, forever
      shining bright, hidden
in my own little world.

auctioneer

going once, going twice,
Sold! to the young woman
with the smeared rose lipstick
and red-rimmed eyes, a scowling smile
that spoke a thousand goodbyes,
for the heart she once guarded
is of no use anymore,
so why not bargain for a
dagger to win this war?

EVERY TEEN MOVIE

girl meets boy;
love at first sight, nothing will ever be the same
so
girl unravels, morphs, chisels away at herself
(the stone ballerina refigured into a lump of
clay)
because she is suddenly inadequate,
unworthy of attention unless the glasses are
discarded
because of course contacts are superior, just
don't
stab your eye out after he's broken your heart
after the honeymoon phase has dwindled
like the remnants of a raging fire,
only smothering ashes
left behind.

Rules of an Introvert

One: say nothing, ghostly silhouette
drifting through time and space, an outsider
behind the looking glass.

Two: do nothing, simply watch
the sunset, fading colors glanced at
for seconds, then forgotten; our fate.

Three: be nothing, emptiness
swallowing itself whole, where echoes
of screaming souls lie buried, stifled.

Rule Four:

Self-Sabotage

I don't want to be your metaphor,
The reason for your life's failures.

The depth of my friendship was not an ocean,
stretching to infinity,
and it was not my yearning for authenticity that
dragged us down
and anchored our relationship to the murky sea
floor,
but rather your lack thereof.

I don't want to be your metaphor,
the girl in the story who ruined your life,
because that was never me, so
maybe you can claim self-sabotage instead.

You

You are the rain,
a melodic cacophony of music
humming outside my rusty window,
infiltrating the thoughts in my brain.

(i don't know what happens next but—

You fell from the sky, unexpected,
yet I smiled and drew my blanket closer
and warmed my hands against a teacup,
comforted by your presence and our
oh, so sweet connection.

—with you, I am not invisible—

You are the storm, naturally occurring,
that changed the way I see myself,
the raging lightning and gentle thunder
instilling confidence, self-love,
the knowledge that I am a masterpiece
still stirring.

—and for that, I thank you)

This Morning

this morning i took a walk around campus with music blasting in my ears, a canvas bag slung across my body as my wild curls swayed with the wind, while sunlight refracted through leaves that couldn't decide what color they wanted to be, and i danced and sang as i weaved between mud puddles and graffiti tunnels and towering trees, each whispering their own stories into the air i breathed. and this morning when i found myself retracing my steps and twirling carefree, there was a horse staring at me, and so i approached the gate and let her sniff my hand, then stroked her chestnut coat ever so gently. as she plodded away to continue her graze, i took the path home with a smiling soul.

Where I am From

Where are you from? is the kind of question
that leaves me breathless, a weighted blanket
encompassing my mind, body, and soul—

am i from my mother's land?
The republic of salty sea, battered red flags, tales
of Baba Yaga
which others incorrectly inquire as being "near
atlanta?"

am i from this place I was not born in
yet exhale with every breath,
culture steeped like tea into the fiber of my
being
though the language, i barely speak?

it could be
that i am from the states i have lived in
but which one rings truer to myself?

am i from the snowy hilltops of pennsylvania,
of temperamental weather and pierogies and
yinz
a place in which i left and then returned

or am i from the indiana cornfields,
suspiciously devoid of bugs?

am i from deep in the heart of texas,
of crawfish festivals and cowboy hats and
gun-wielding restaurant goers?
or virginia, where i will spend my next few
years?

perhaps, if nothing else, i am simply a collection
of my experiences.